BECOMING PRAYER

JEAN-PIERRE DUBOIS-DUMÉE

Becoming Prayer

St Paul Publications

Original title: *La Prière. Pourquoi? Comment?*

Translated from the French by Anne White

Cover design: Mary Lou Winters FSP

Photos: © Epipress: Pino p. 3; Angelo del Canale p. 42

M. L. Winters pp. 13, 23, 31, 51, 59, 64-65

St Paul Publications
Middlegreen, Slough SL3 6BT, England

First published in Great Britain 1989
Printed and bound by Dotesios Printers Ltd, Trowbridge, Wiltshire
ISBN 085439 311 0

St Paul Publications is an activity of the priests and brothers of the Society of St Paul who proclaim the Gospel through the media of social communication

Contents

1

Becoming prayer 6

2

Christian prayer 12

3

How Jesus prayed 16

4

Asking, thanking, adoring 22

5

The great prayers 30

6

What's the use of praying 42

7

The sources of prayer 50

8

The advice of Jesus 58

9

Resources 66

1

Becoming prayer

When you ask someone if he prays, the answer is generally: "very little", or "morning and evening", or "the Our Father and the Hail Mary". Some people say: "I've done my prayers", rather in the tone in which you might say: "I've finished my washing-up". People often blur the distinction between "prayer" and "prayers".

To fail to pray is to leave God out of our existence, and not just God, but everything that God signifies for the world he has created, the world in which we live.

Archbishop Anthony Bloom

Prayers are ways to God: they are paths, or stages, though undeniably necessary; they are means put into our hands by the religious tradition to which we belong. They are things to do.

Prayer however is something deeper. It is a state of being; you can talk of a "state of prayer" just as you can talk of a "state of grace". And, moreover, it is a way of life, and it is this which gives life to "prayers", gives them, as it were, a guarantee of their authenticity and the power of love.

Let us pray that the Lord implant in us something that he can make use of.

Teilhard de Chardin to Jeanne Mortier

What is asked of us, therefore, is not so much that we "say prayers" as that we "live in prayer", constantly in the presence of God, so that we become one huge longing for God, so that we "become prayer".

To pray is to love

To get there, we have to establish a relationship, a personal encounter with God. It is

not so much a "lifting-up" towards a distant God, as an intimacy with a God who is there at the deepest level of our being, a God who is waiting for us, a God who is listening to us, even though he apparently only reveals himself in silence. It is a God who loves us, and whom we love: praying and loving are the same.

This personal relationship can lead to a kind of union. We aren't trying to work on a God who is external to us when we start praying, and make him come to us. We are seeking to contemplate a God who is already within us, and to unite ourselves to him. Hence we find so many prayers of love, like those of St Gertrude, or of abandonment, like those of Charles of Jesus, Fr Charles de Foucauld, who used to say: "the best prayer is the one where there is the most love".

God often calls on us; but most of the time we are not at home.

John Tauler (14th century mystic)

So we're talking about mystical prayer, you might say. And why not? Prayer has a mystical aspect in so far as it goes beyond a relationship of the heart or the mind to God. You sometimes find that committed Christians are a bit hesitant about the "mystical", because they immediately start thinking about extraordinary phenomena like visions or levitation. But mysticism is an uncomplicated and desperate longing to have God present in our lives.

Prayer and faith

Seen in this light, prayer goes hand-in-hand with faith in God: but the corollary of this is that there is no real faith without prayer, i.e., without a relationship between us and God; otherwise faith would be just a spiritual thing, with no flesh or vitality to it.

Is it not a peculiar contradiction that people can totally believe in God and yet pray to him so little, and so badly?

George Bernanos

Prayer is...

- The raising up of the soul to God (*John Damascene*, eighth century)
- Simply, union with God (*Curé d'Ars*)
- A conversation with a friend; and that includes knowing how to shut up and listen (*St Ignatius of Loyola*)
- A conversation with God (*Gregory of Nyssa*, fourth century)
- The key to Holy Writ (*Isaac the Syrian*, seventh century)
- A heart-to-heart talk, in which the soul flows into God and God flows into the soul, in order to transform it into himself (*Elizabeth of the Trinity*)
- Awakening to God's presence within (*James Borst*)
- Full attentiveness (*Simone Weil*)
- A one-word description of a life-time's journey into God (*Delia Smith*)
- Prayer isn't a matter of a lot of thinking; it's a lot of loving (*St Teresa of Avila*)
- Prayer is a way of life... an attitude to living and breathing... an awareness of God in all our experiences, good and bad (*Frank Topping*)
- It is a matter of opening yourself to God, just as you open yourself to the fire, or to the sun or to the light (*Louis Evely*)
- Your prayer is God's word of longing and love in you, God's breathing of the Spirit in you, to make you want the union he wants (*Maria Boulding*)

Prayer and faith feed each other. You pray because you believe in God; although sometimes you find yourself praying to a God you don't believe in, or in whom your faith isn't all that strong, simply to obtain faith. You pray in order to find God. Prayer is a homing device.

In his 1978 "Notebooks", Albert Cohen, a writer brought up in Judaism, but now an atheist, published some Psalms which are real cries of defiance: "One last time, I tell You that I want to believe in You... Show me that You love me, help me to believe in spite of my blasphemy and my mockery... Have pity on this unbeliever who hasn't the good fortune to have had the faith passed down to him. I am only waiting on You in order to believe. Is it a sin to wait only for You?"

Prayer is not a burden, but a gift; it is not a constraint, but a freedom; it is not a millstone round our neck, but a source of joy.

Pope John Paul II

Finally, prayer and faith are like two hands joined. Faith isn't a thing you possess, a pebble to grasp in your hands, it's both a quest and a conquest, which you are forever having to start all over again; and prayer is both the expression of this and its instrument.

And just as you can't separate prayer from faith, so you can't separate it from thought, from feeling, from action, or from the will. It is not a separate area, or a desert island: it is a dimension of all our human activity, a way of being. There's no point in trying to stick it onto the outside of our lives, because it's already, at least in embryo, there in our hearts, at the very deepest level of our being.

A Pharaoh of Egypt

How many are your creations,
Hidden from the sight of man.
O only God, to whom no other is like,
You have created the earth in accordance with your desires...
How powerful are your designs, O Lord of eternity.

Akhenaton (Egypt ca. 1350 BC)

The Opening lines of the Koran

Praise to You, Lord of the Worlds,
The merciful, the compassionate,
The King of Judgement Day.
It is you whom we adore,
You whose help we implore.

The *Gloria* of the early Christians

Benefactor of all those who turn to you,
Light of all those who are in darkness,
Creating principle of all seeds,
Gardener of all spiritual growth,
Have pity on me, Lord,
Make of me a spotless temple.
Do not look at my sins.
If you take account of my faults
I shall no longer be able to endure your presence;
but by your immense mercy
and your infinite compassion,
wipe away my stains
through Our Lord Jesus Christ,
your most holy only child,
healer of our souls.
Through him all glory, power, honour, and magnificence to you,
through the ages upon ages that never grow old
or come to an end. Amen!

2

Christian Prayer

There are men and women at prayer everywhere you look

In the Cairo Museum, I met a Muslim keeper telling his beads before going to prostrate himself at the Mosque. At the Wailing Wall in Jerusalem I saw Jews reciting Psalms swaying like pendulums. I have heard them singing in Aramaic, the language that Christ spoke. At the foot of the pyramids, I have read the amazing prayer of Pharaoh Akhenaton to the only God. I have heard the moving prayers of the Sumerians, 4,000 years before Christ, and of the Hittites of Mesopotamia. I have prayed the Inca peasants' prayer to the Most High God, and meditated with the help of Veda texts from India. I have sung Negro spirituals and recited Morning Prayer using the words of African animists.

In all places, since the beginning of time, people have prayed; not always, it is true, as I pray – but I can't judge their fervour on those grounds. In their formulations I have found many blessings, many expressions of adoration and appeals for mercy, and many expressions of solidarity with other human beings (along with occasional manifestations of intolerance, it must be admitted); I have also found in other religions a profound sense of sin, and even the idea of waiting for a Saviour or hoping for a kingdom of tenderness, justice and peace.

**At this very moment,
in all the earth,
there are Christians,
Jews, Muslims, and
Buddhists at prayer.
I do not suppose
that a single second
goes by when there
is not a human soul
in prayer...
We are not alone.
Everywhere you find
the peace that
prayer brings,
the glimmerings
of grace, the Church
of souls.
We are a people of
tiny quiet flames,
burning at night,
which get lit from
each other,
and spread through
the darkness.**

Petru Dimitriu

"It is from you, Lord, that I hope for forgiveness for my faults on Judgement Day; grant me wisdom, do not put me in a sad lot on the Day of Resurrection." This prayer is taken, not from the Bible, but from the Koran. "Come to me, O God, and take care of me. Outside of you nothing means anything to me. You are the only one, come back to me, O God, day after day." You might have thought that came from the Psalms, but it is an invocation to the Sun-God, in Egypt, and it dates from the second millennium BC.

We may think that our prayers come out of our heads, but in fact they come out of the presence of God praying in our souls.

Hubert Van Zeller

And the Christian tradition too has its share of selfish or ineptly addressed prayers, or horrifying curses such as we cheerfully criticise in other religions. So what is specifically Christian in this global phenomenon which we call prayer?

Our prayer is the prayer of Christ in us

Our prayer is that which Christ addresses in us to his Father, and which we make our own with the help of the Holy Spirit. Christian prayer is prayer to God the Father, through the Son, in the Spirit. Hence the way in which we frequently start or finish our prayers: "In the name of the Father, and of the Son, and of the Holy Spirit." The Spirit is the gift which comes to the help of our weakness (Rom 8:26-27). He himself intercedes for us: "He guides us from within," writes Pope John Paul II, "he is present in our prayer, and he gives it a divine dimension."

The heart of our prayer, or the prayer of our heart, is, above all, a prayer of love, a prayer of thanksgiving, a prayer of adoration. But we suffocate this prayer through all the things that weigh us down; selfishly, we turn it towards ourselves, instead of turning it to God; we are neither sufficiently transparent, nor sufficiently generous. Christian prayer does not confer any rights, for it is a grace, a gift, which is Christ himself. Any obstacle comes from us, and from us alone.

This is why we have to pray to the Father "in his name". We do not insist nearly enough on these three words when we quote those well-known sayings: "Whatever you ask in my name, I will do it... If you ask anything of the Father, he will give it to you in my name. Hitherto you have asked nothing in my name". What defines Christian prayer is, simply, to pray "in the name of Christ".

Before ever it is a means to an end, prayer is the expression of what I have become by grace. I do not pray in order to enter the kingdom of God, but because God has freely given me entry into his kingdom. I pray because Christ has brought me into the Father's presence.

Mgr Coffy

Praying doesn't change God: it changes us

This is the source of all those things that make Christian prayer Christian: confidence, love, grace, forgiveness (for that is God's special characteristic), a sense of solidarity with others (for having one Father means that we are all brothers and sisters, a pilgrim people), and a sense of waiting for the salvation that Jesus brings.

We don't change God by praying (that's pagan prayer); prayer changes us, with the help of the Holy Spirit. St John says: "In this is love, not that we loved God but that he loved us." Because of his love, God puts himself last and gives us everything. It is up to us to let him bring into being what he loves about us. It is up to us to make ready for the kingdom and to start building it here and now.

Our prayer is God's work, God's creation. As you kneel there, sit there, walk about or whatever you do when you pray you are saying "Yes" with your whole being to his will that you should be, that you should be you, that you should be united to him.

Maria Boulding

3

How Jesus prayed

Since all Christian prayer is based on Jesus Christ, it may be as well to examine the gospel in order to meet Christ in prayer. He is not merely the messenger of prayer, he is himself the message, and the heart of the message. He is not merely the master of prayer, he is the heart of prayer.

"Not my will but thine"

Sometimes it seems a little odd that prayer does not have a more prominent place in the evangelists' recital. We see Jesus preaching, teaching, and healing, but it is far more rarely that we see him praying.

In fact, of course, it could hardly be otherwise. His prayer is the most private part of him. Even the apostles themselves only got the chance to pray with him on rare occasions. And when the chance was offered they snored their way through it! As, no doubt, we should have done. As we do today, because we lack the skill or the will to stay awake with him.

At the Mount of Olives, in the moment of Jesus' greatest distress and his greatest testing, he said to the disciples who had accompanied him: "So, could you not watch with me one hour?" A stinging rebuke which finds an echo in each one of us.
He adds: "Watch and pray that you may not

**And being in an agony he prayed more earnestly...
And when he rose from prayer, he came to his disciples and found them sleeping for sorrow, and he said to them, "Why do you sleep? Rise up and pray that you may not enter into temptation".**

Luke 22: 44-46

Пріидите
комнѣ вси
труждаю
щіися и о
бремене
нніи и азъ
упокою

enter into temptation" (Mt 26:36-46; Mk 14:32-42; Lk 22:34-47). The temptation he speaks of is the temptation to sleep, to despair, which, as Peguy said, is the most serious temptation of all. You might have thought that Christ was on the point of giving into that temptation when he asked for the chalice to be removed from him. But when he prayed again, he added: "Nevertheless, not my will but thine be done". So the heart of prayer, and the source of the Incarnation, is surrender to the Father's will. That is why we can call Jesus, "prayer made man".

At this decisive moment of his passion, there is also an echo of the "Our Father", with the same familiar form of address: "Abba" (in Mark), and the same concern that God's will be done. It is very much the essential element in prayer, as John frequently insists in what he has preserved of Christ's remarks: "my food is to do the will of him who sent me" (Jn 4:34).

Prayer is twofold.
It is an insatiable taste of that which we seek, and it will give us the courage to say "yes" to the next devastating situation that comes along, the next stepping stone to union on the cross which he, the Carpenter, has fashioned for each one of us individually.

Catherine de Hueck Doherty

In John's Gospel

It is John who gives the best account of Christ's way of proceeding, in one of the best known passages of his gospel, the one known as the "Priestly Prayer" of Jesus. It is a prayer of intercession, which the evangelist places in the course of Christ's last evening (it forms the whole of chapter 17 of his gospel); but more than that, it is a prayer that sums up the whole of Jesus' life. It is a prayer of loving and being loved, of self-offering, of "Thou" and "I", of confidence and of praise. It is a prayer about the kingdom, a prayer of eternal life, a prayer of unity in love. It is a model for, or, if you like, a foreshadowing of, our own prayer. "The underlying experience of Jesus in prayer was the relationship of Son to Father, Son to "Abba". The redemptive union of the Christian with Christ means nothing less than that experience is open to each one of us" (John Dalrymple, *The Cross a Pasture*).

Starting with this extraordinary text from John (see the extracts on p. 21) gives one a fresh insight into all the other places where the evangelists refer to Jesus' prayer. Here we are getting a glimpse of what Jesus said when he prayed. The next question is: when did he do it? Quite simply: at all the key moments of his mission.

At all the key moments

Jesus prays at the moment when he receives the baptism of John the Baptist (Lk 3:21-22). It is often Luke who talks about the prayer of Jesus. And immediately the Father-Son relationship is affirmed by the voice that comes from heaven: "You are my Son".

Jesus prays at the moment when his mission of preaching throughout Galilee is inaugurated (Mk 1:35).

He prays at the moment when he picks his team of twelve disciples (Lk 6:12).

He prays at the end of one of his most important miracles, the multiplication of the loaves (Mk 6:46; Lk 9:18).

He prays at the time of the Transfiguration (Lk 9:28).

He is praying just before the moment when the disciples, seeing him at prayer, ask him

Jesus prays before and after doing anything, be it preaching or healing.

The first stage is to retire, whenever he gets the chance, into the solitude of a desert or a mountain. The second step is that they come and call him out of the solitude: "Everyone is searching for you" (Mark 1:37). He comes back to people, to everyday life; he shares their concerns. "But so much the more the report went abroad concerning him; and great multitudes gathered to hear and to be healed of their infirmities" (Luke 5:15). After that he goes off again, and this is the third step, finding his Father in prayer once more: "But he withdrew to the wilderness and prayed" (Luke 5:16).

So there is a constant to-and-fro from prayer to action, and from action to prayer.

to teach them how they should do it, and he gives them the "Our Father" (Lk 11:1).

He prays at the moment of the institution of the Eucharist – he gives thanks (Mt 26:27; Mk 14:23; Lk 22:17,19).

He prays for Peter, just before Peter's denial of him (Lk 22:32).

He prays, as we have seen, at Gethsemane, but also he prays for his executioners on Calvary (Lk 23:34), and to be faithful to his own mission: "My God, my God, why hast thou forsaken me?" (Mk 15:34; cf. also Mt 26:36) and "Father, into thy hands I commit my spirit" (Lk 23:46).

Jesus prayed a great deal, for he lived in constant dialogue with his Father. But the disciples never saw it; they only preserved the great occasions. Normally on these occasions, Jesus went off apart. He withdrew into the mountains. He withdrew from the crowd in order to go and rediscover his Father. He made a retreat, as it were; not in order to forget his mission, but in order to have strength to accomplish it, whatever the cost.

Christ's prayer before his Passion

(Extracts from John 17)

Father, the hour has come; glorify thy Son that thy Son may glorify thee.

I have manifested thy name to the men whom thou gavest me...

Now they know that everything that thou hast given me is from thee...

Sanctify them in the truth; thy word is truth...

Even as thou, Father, art in me, and I in thee, that they also may be in us, so that the world may believe that thou hast sent me.

O Righteous Father... I made known to them thy name, and I will make it known, that the love with which thou hast loved me may be in them, and I in them.

4

Asking, thanking, adoring

There are many ways of praying, but in the end they all There are many ways of praying, but in the end they all meet up in the desire to welcome God into the deepest level of one's being. The kingdom has several entrances, and each of us must find his own.

The prayer of petition

You cannot just ask for any odd thing

This is the most common form of prayer, and the most instinctive; praying, for example, to obtain a cure for some sickness, or success in an exam, or for some undertaking to go well; or again it might be a retreat from unhappiness, the end of a drought, or the punishment of the wicked. This is precisely what pagans used to do when, under the influence of fear or suffering, they turned to their idols: "Scratch my back, and I'll scratch yours."

We shouldn't be surprised at this. The word "pray" originally means to "ask for", and in any case, a prayer of this sort, self-interested though it may be, starts off by recognizing our weakness and poverty; it is too easy to make fun of it.

Did not Christ declare: "Ask, and it will be given you" (Mt 7:7; Lk 11:9); and again: "Whatever you ask in prayer, you will re-

Prayer of petition calls for the greatest courage. Faith comes into the open, exposes itself, commits itself.

Anthony de Mello SJ

My prayers, my God, flow from what I am not; I think thy answers make me what I am.

George MacDonald

God's essential answer to every petition is himself, and this answer may not always be expressed in precisely the way that we had hoped or wanted.

Simon Tugwell

ceive, if you have faith" (Mt 21:22). On the other hand, he also said, immediately afterwards: "but let your will be done, and not mine". On a number of occasions he made it a bit more specific: "Whatever you ask in my name, I will do it" (Jn 14:14). And he even says "Whatever you ask in prayer, believe that you receive it, and you will" (Mk 11:24).

Let us pray that the Lord may place in us that which enables him to make use of us.

Teilhard de Chardin

You can't just ask for any old thing. God is not a penny-in-the-slot machine. He doesn't give us things that we could choose for ourselves or that the laws of nature can give us. What he wants us to ask for is not healing but patience, not good fortune but courage, not luck but love and fraternal solidarity. Margaret Hebblethwaite writes: "What I want and desire is somewhere between petitions for my consciously-felt, minor, earthly wants, and the higher desires that are not yet mine. Prayer happens in the tension between the two" (*Finding God in All Things*). As St Paul observed: "For we do not know how to pray as we ought" (Rom 8:26).

Pray, but not (as we normally do) to ask that God hears you: it is you who must hear God, as you well know.

A Quaker Text

Cardinal Hume notes one important result of our prayer: "God is in touch with us, as friends can be in touch, making known to us what he wants of us" (*To be a Pilgrim*). And that's what gives us the desire and the duty to take steps to gain entry into the kingdom defined by the Beatitudes.

There are some people who worry about their gardens, and others worry about the grassland, others about the pigs, and others because they no longer have anything to put in their pasties. These prayers that you are attempting to make God listen to are prayers for beans, petitions for tomatoes; they are alleluias for artichokes and hosannas for pumpkins. All that is cupboard love. That can't make it up to heaven; it can no more fly than a plucked turkey can.

Sermon of a French parish priest about a spring that dried up

The prayer of thanksgiving

This is apparently the complete opposite of the previous type: no longer do we say "please", but "thank you". But still there is the same underlying question: what are you giving thanks for? Not for riches, success, or luck. What about the wonders of nature? All right, but what are we to say about earthquakes and volcanoes? There are people who regard disasters of this sort as a reason for not believing in the God whom we proclaim to be good and merciful.

More than just saying "thank you"

Our act of thanksgiving is a leap into the beyond. Let us note, first, that it is much more than just saying "thank you". It is an act, which means that it is not just a passive and belated "thanks", but something we do. It means doing our bit in the hymn of creation to its creator, a commitment now and for the future to growth in Christian life. For grace, which is a gift, calls for a gracious giving thanks: we both respond to what has happened and wait for the next move, working to build a better world. Thanking is a very religious act: people often talk about "returning" thanks, giving back what one has received, giving it a new start, spreading it about.

And what we have received is not this, that or the other benefit: it is God himself. We thank God for existing and for having shown us his love. "O give thanks to the Lord, for he is good, for his steadfast love endures for ever", says Psalm 136, as we sing readily enough. Everything is in this prayer, especially when you realize that God's love is ex-

You pray in your distress and your need: would that you might also pray in the fullness of your joy and in your days of abundance.

Kahlil Gibran

From St Paul:

Thanks be to God, through Jesus Christ our Lord.

Romans 7:26

Thanks be to God for his inexpressible gift!

2 Corinthians 9:15

I thank him who has given me strength for this, Christ Jesus our Lord.

1 Timothy 1:12

Sing psalms
and hymns
and spiritual songs
with thankfulness
in your hearts to God.

Colossians 3:16

Give thanks in
all circumstances;
for this is the will
of God in Christ Jesus
for you.

1 Thessalonians 5:18

pressed in the Incarnation of Jesus Christ who is by our side, leading us on the way to salvation.

AT MASS

There is thanksgiving all the way through the Eucharistic celebration, of which we have not perhaps taken sufficient notice.
In the Gloria*: "We give you thanks for your great glory."*
In the Preface*: "We do well always and everywhere to give you thanks."*
At the Sanctus*: "Blessed is he" (which is a form of thanksgiving).*
At the Consecration: *"He took bread... gave you thanks..."*

"Father, I give you thanks"

When we pray like this, we are imitating the attitude of Jesus himself, who unceasingly gives thanks to his Father. This is the heart of his prayer, in so far as you can see it through the gospels. "I thank thee, Father, Lord of heaven and earth, that thou hast hidden these things from the wise and understanding and revealed them to babes" (Mt 11:25). "Father, I thank thee that thou hast heard me. I know that thou hearest me always" (Jn 11:41). When Jesus takes the seven loaves and the fish, he gives thanks (Mt 15:36), and he does the same at the Last Supper. The whole of Jesus' prayer, and the whole of his life, is a thanksgiving.

The more man
becomes man,
the more he will
feel a need, which
becomes increasingly
more explicit,
more discriminating
and more wanton,
for love.

Teilhard de Chardin

And we too need to live in an atmosphere of thanksgiving, not so much for this or that benefit or success, but for faith and for love: God's faith and love, and Christ's, and the faith and love of all those who live in imitation of Jesus, that is to say, all the saints of yesterday and of today.

Prayer of adoration

I love you

This is the most contemplative aspect of prayer; and that word, "contemplative", ought not to throw us into a panic, for there is no Christian life of any depth without looking at God, or at least a desire to contemplate. It is the same with the love of God as with the love between a man and a woman: there is a way of approaching the other, of welcoming him or her, of looking at the other, which does not necessarily require words. The Curé d'Ars used to say: "what bliss it is to love God".

Adoration! That word comes from heaven; one can define it as the ecstasy of love: love crushed by the beauty, the strength, the utter grandeur of the one loved.

Elizabeth of the Trinity

From adoration it is but a short step to praise. You find it in the Old Testament, in the prayers of Moses, David and Judith, and especially in some of the Psalms. It is also in the New Testament: sometimes, as in the *Benedictus*, in the form of blessing; sometimes, as in the *Magnificat*, in the form of exaltation. Also in this category are hymns like the Christmas *Gloria*. But this idea of the "glory of God" sometimes gets misunderstood, as when it is identified with omnipotence. The glory of God is not of the same order of things as an eye-catching victory. The glory of God is in loving and being loved.

**O Thou who art
infinitely good,
infinitely loving,
infinitely great,
infinitely simple,
utterly immutable,
Eternal,
All-powerful,
infinitely Merciful,
Strong and Sweet,
Intelligent, Wise,
Perfect, Holy,
I adore Thee.**

Extract from the prayer of adoration, Bethlehem Monasteries

I seek your face

However, it should not be supposed that this prayer of adoration or this song of praise is easy: in prayer we travel hopefully, rather than arrive; we yearn for it, but do not possess it. It is a very striking observation that the great "adorers of God", such as Augustine or Ambrose or Teresa of Avila, are always seeking for the God who is love. Their motto is taken from the Psalms: "I seek your face". So Augustine writes in his *De Trinitate*: "So far as I was able, I searched for you: I have not ceased from searching for you. Grant that I may always gaze ardently on your face. Give me the strength to search for you, you who have given me the hope of finding you". In this sense, it is certain that those Christians who are apparently assured of their Christianity are not inevitably the closest to God; whereas non-Christians, in their search for God, are often very close to him. You cannot judge from the outside what goes on in the secret places of the heart.

**I seek your face,
O Lord. Do not hide
your face from me.
Henceforth, O Thou,
my Lord and my God,
teach me at the
deepest level
of my heart, where
and how I must
seek you, where and
how I am to find you.
If you are not within
me, where am I
to look for you?
But if you are present
everywhere, how is it
that I cannot see you?**

***St Anselm
(12th century)***

The prayer of repentance: an appeal for forgiveness

Sorry!

This is a prayer in which we recognise that we are sinners, an appeal to the mercy of God: "Lord, have mercy", and at the same time we show forgiveness towards others, for there is a link between the pardon we receive and the pardon we give. There is no real prayer, no surge of love, without this recognition that we are sinners, without this humility and this poverty. From the earliest centuries, Christians were thought of as "forgiveness people".

**Have mercy on me,
O God, according
to thy steadfast love;
according to
thy abundant mercy
blot out my
transgressions.**

Psalm 50

One and the same prayer

So this rapid analysis makes it clear to us that the main kinds of prayer (and we could add many others) are not mutually exclusive categories. We cannot confidently give adoration to God without becoming aware of our sinfulness. If we adore God, inevitably we find in ourselves the desire to give thanks to him; inevitably we find ourselves asking him to help us find our way into the kingdom. Asking, giving thanks, adoration, praise, repentance, are not separate moments or stages of prayer; these are the indivisible and convergent elements of one and the same prayer, which ultimately consists in living in the presence of God, welcoming him at the deepest level of our being, leaving it all to him, leaving ourselves in his hands.

If we confess our sins, he is faithful and just, and will forgive our sins and cleanse us from all unrighteousness.

1 John 1:9

Each one has his own way in

The main thing is to enter into prayer, whether it's by way of asking humbly, by way of thanksgiving, or adoration or repentance, or joy or tenderness, or abandonment or wonder or deference, attentiveness or watchfulness, sharing your state of distress, or even impatience. For everyone, depending on what is happening outside or inside them, one or other of these doors is always open to them: the Kingdom is always there, waiting for you, whole and entire, behind your particular door.

Find the door of your heart, and you will find the door of the kingdom of God.

St John Chrysostom

There are also different kinds of prayer: prayer to God the Father, prayer to Jesus, the Son, prayer to the Spirit, prayer to Mary, prayer to the saints.

The first three are linked, just as the three persons of the Trinity are linked. Prayer to Mary and the saints are more accurately described as prayer with them: they are companions on the road, who can perform great services for us; so different are they, and sometimes so close to us!

5

The great prayers

The "Our Father": the prayer Jesus taught us

The basic and irreplaceable prayer

This is the prayer that Christ himself taught us, thereby associating us with his own prayer to the Father, within the Trinity. It is only quoted by Matthew and Luke (Mt 6:9-13; Lk 11:2-4), with one or two small differences, but the main ideas, such as the Fatherhood of God, forgiveness, and bread, are scattered throughout the other two gospels also.

A prayer for the coming of the kingdom of heaven

This kingdom is the one depicted both in the Beatitudes and in the parables. The Lord's Prayer is, as it were, the Beatitudes in prayer form, and the two must always be taken together.

The Christian prayer par excellence

The Lord's Prayer is *the* prayer of the Christian. In the early Church it was a sort of privilege to say the "Our Father. In fact catechumens were allowed to say it only after their Baptism. It was a kind of sign, or badge, that one was a Christian. Subsequently, the

The Lord's Prayer cannot be understood apart from the whole ministry and teaching of Jesus.
Its significance is unfolded as Jesus moves forward in his work: there is revealed the meaning of the words around which the Lord's Prayer centres – the Father,
the name,
the kingdom,
the will.

Michael Ramsey
Former Archbishop of Canterbury

אבא

ABBA

hen you are praying, do not behave
ke the hypocrites who love to stand
nd pray in synagogues or on street
rners in order to be noticed. I give you
y word, they are already repaid.
henever you pray, go to your room,
ose your door, and pray to your Father
private. Then your Father who sees
hat no man sees, will repay you. In
our prayer do not rattle on like the
agans. They think they will win a hear-
g by the sheer multiplication of words.
o not imitate them. Your Father knows
hat you need before you ask him. This
how you are to pray:
ur Father in heaven, hallowed be your
ame, your kingdon come, your will be
one on earth as it is in heaven. Give us
day our daily bread, and forgive us
e wrong we have done as we forgive
ose who wrong us. Subject us not to
e trial but deliver us from the evil one.

"Our Father" became an integral part of the Eucharistic celebration. Its importance stems from the fact that Jesus himself taught us this prayer.

More than just a prayer

What matters isn't just the words. What the disciples asked was not "give us a prayer" but "teach us to pray". So the Lord's Prayer is not just the model prayer, it is how you pray: it gives us a way to prayer. It is an apprenticeship in praying, the best possible introduction to the art of praying.

We often say
the "Our Father"
too quickly.
It is like washing
when fully clothed,
with a little water
in the hollow of
your hands.

Alexander Solzhenytsin

A prayer entrusted to us

This prayer has come down the centuries. It has been entrusted to us, from generation to generation, as you pass on a secret, or like the baton in a relay race. It has been transmitted to us, and it is up to us to transmit it onwards. What would be left of Christianity if we had forgotten the "Our Father"?

Stage One: Invocation

It's all there right from the beginning. The first words stake out a sense of wonder, the start of the process of adoration: you are our Father, we love you. One ought almost to say "Daddy" or "Beloved Father", because the Aramaic word "Abba" (which you find elsewhere in the gospel) gives it an intimate feeling which has no parallel in other religious traditions.

However, we are not to forget that this Father is more than just an earthly father. The expression "who art in heaven" is not meant to signify an address, but the special nature of this God, who is at one and the same time

Our Father in heaven,
we honour your holy
name. We ask that
your kingdom will
come now. May your
will be done here on
earth, just as it is
in heaven.
Give us our food again
today, as usual, and
forgive us our sins,
just as we have
forgiven those who
have sinned against
us. Don't bring us
into temptation,
but deliver us from
the Evil One. Amen.

Living Bible Version
Matthew 6: 9-13

both very close indeed and quite other, wholly transcendent, the creator of the universe.

Finally, once God is recognized as Father, we are all (and jolly well should be) brothers and sisters, whatever our class, race or religion.

You can say the words "Our Father" mechanically, like a robot, without thinking at all. Then the words fall silent... they are "by heart", but no longer speak to the heart... Or you can say the words like a secret, like a way of saying: I love you. Then the words take on a freshness and a gleaming newness, which make your heart flower again.

Jean Debruynne

Stage Two: Evocation

These next three petitions hang together and complete each other. They would be meaningless if the petitions were for God: we can add nothing to the Heavenly Father's kingdom. It is more of a vision, whose function is to make us play our part in the building of the kingdom here below, "on earth as in heaven". Insufficient emphasis has been given to this expression, which probably relates to all three definitions of the kingdom at once (the hallowed name, the promised kingdom, and the will that is done are all "on earth as in heaven"), and which gives us a good idea of the meaning of the whole of the Lord's Prayer and its urgency: it is to start here and now (a little later we say: give us this day). In this second stage, we address God in the second person (thy name, thy kingdom, thy will) because we wish to give expression to our love.

You know, when I recite the "Our Father" and say "give us this day our daily bread", it is as though I were saying "give me the love and tenderness I need."

A young person

Stage Three: Our vocation

What are the conditions we need to meet in order to build this kingdom? At this point we are no longer addressing the Father; the emphasis is on us. It is all about our mission. What we are asking for is bread (both physical, and the bread of life which John's gospel talks about), forgiveness (so difficult and so vital in Christianity), and freedom from the sin which prevents us from helping to build the kingdom here below.

The "Our Father" is very much a prayer that engages us and defines us, a prayer for today. Pope John Paul II has called it "a prayer to change the world". It remains to be seen whether or not we make it too ordinary, too mechanical, or too glib.

The "Hail Mary": the great standby

The opening words are those of Gabriel, as we find them in Luke's gospel. About the fourth or fifth century this greeting was linked with Elizabeth's when Mary came to see her: "You are blessed among women...". For a long time, these two greetings were the whole of the prayer to Mary, and this prayer got developed or paraphrased (this is the origin of the litanies). It was only at the end of the thirteenth century that this prayer came into the liturgy. But the second part, the invocations, hardly appeared before the sixteenth century.

Some people have reservations about the English text (what about all those "thee's" and "thou's" for example?), but it is rooted in tradition, and there is no fundamental reason to modify it. However, there have been one or two attempts, such as the following: "Rejoice, Mary, filled with joy, you are blessed among women, and Jesus, your child, is blessed. Holy Mary, Mother of God, pray for us sinners, now and when we die". However you present it, the "Hail Mary" is a basic prayer. Peguy said that he sometimes found it difficult to recite the Lord's Prayer and mean it ("thy will be done", for instance); but in those circumstances, he said, "I used to pray to Mary. The Marian prayers are great

Without Mary, the knowledge of Christ remains on the level of pure speculation; but in Mary it becomes experiential, because it takes on the humility and the poverty without which it is impossible to know Christ. Mary's holiness is the silence in which Christ can be heard.

Thomas Merton

Mary herself is one of the Creator's most merciful thoughts. It is all there in the "Hail Mary". With Gabriel we recognize and love the highest when we see it in Mary's human nature, raised to such destiny. With the Church we feel sure that since she is Mother of God's Son, he will be glad to be approached through her.

F. H. Drinkwater

standbys. There isn't one of them that the most dreadful sinner could not pray and mean. In the mechanics of salvation, the *Ave Maria* is the bottom line. With that, you can't be lost".

We need not be astonished that this extremely simple prayer should have developed into the Rosary. People talk about an "infantile droning", but if you meditate the Rosary, it ceases to be "by heart", and becomes instead a "heart to heart", blossoming out into contemplation. Robert Llewelyn, chaplain of the Julian shrine in Walsingham, the national shrine of Our Lady in England, has written: "We move from one 'Hail Mary' to the next with such devotion as God may give us, and then there may be, as it were, a short period on the wing, when the words though still recited, recede into the background, and somehow we are taken beyond them, and held for a few moments in that stillness which is God" (*A Doorway into Silence*).

And if you use the Rosary to link it to the life of Christ himself, to the mysteries of Jesus that Mary lived, then you find a kind of mini-gospel, which you can use to reflect on your own life. Pope John Paul II has said: "The fifteen mysteries are fifteen windows through which I look at the events of my life with the eyes of God."

The Psalms

The Book of Psalms is another major form of prayer. Christ prayed them; the gospels often refer to them; they are referred to 360 times in the New Testament as a whole. They have been an inspiration to saints and poets

Praying with Mary means praying the same words that rose from her heart of hearts in response to the angel: "May it be done unto me according to your will."

Brother Roger of Taizé

Each time we name and greet this Mother it is like a solid reference which pulls us up short, like a backlash. Each time we begin the "Hail Mary", we become that angel who calls her by name and we become one in that greeting, with not one movement of her heart or her thought, to the depths of her being, escaping us.

Paul Claudel

alike, and even today they nourish the Church's daily prayer, as well as forming part of the Eucharistic celebration. Some people, however, find them difficult, too far from modern ideas, and too full of violence, and with a thirst for vengeance that doesn't sound at all like the gospel. It is worlds away from the Beatitudes. How can one pray, as Psalm 109 does, "that the children of the wicked become orphans, and his wife a widow"? Sometimes they seem like the prayer-book of the elite; sometimes you feel they belong in a museum, out of date and superseded, as, in a way, the whole of the Old Testament is in comparison to the New Testament.

So should we deprive ourselves of these texts? They are powerful, beautiful, and vigorous, and they express human feelings without any "side" or illusion: you find complaints, imprecations, rebellion, joy, praise. "In the Psalms, human beings have flesh and blood": they shout, and praise, and dance. And we should never forget that the Psalms are meant to be sung.

If you ignore the Psalms, you are cutting out the gospel's "raw material", the heritage from which they spring. It is only natural for people to make their selection in accordance with taste or competence; it is a good idea to go to more accessible translations, such as the Grail Psalms. But, at the end of the day, we may wonder if our task is not to adapt ourselves to them rather than vice versa.

Obviously we have to relate them to the rest of the Old Testament, as it were the prayer book alongside the history book. You don't need a training in biblical exegesis, but only to dip your toe into the idea that, as Yves Congar says, the Psalms are both "the expres-

From the Psalms:

Do not hide
your face from me
in the day of
my distress.
Psalm 102

O Lord, heal me,
for my bones
are troubled.
Psalm 6

Bless the Lord,
O my soul, and all
that is within me,
bless his holy name.
Psalm 103

Rouse thyself!
Why sleepest thou,
O Lord?
Psalm 44

This God,
his way is perfect;
the promise
of the Lord proves
true.
Psalm 18

sion of prayer and a school of prayer". There are keys that we can use to unlock the door; the main key, of course, is Christ himself, chiefly because Christians find his mission, death and resurrection prophetically foreshadowed in the Psalms. And the Psalms can be understood in Christian terms as shouts of praise to the Father. St Augustine says: "It is the one saviour, our Lord Jesus Christ, who prays in us and is prayed to by us. He prays in us as our head. He is prayed to by us as our God. Let us recognise therefore our voices in him and his voice in us."

My God, my God, why hast thou forsaken me.
Psalm 22

Do not cast me off in the time of old age.
Psalm 71

Yes, the shout and the prayer come from me: the external enemies whom the Psalmist complains about are my internal passions. The anguished seeker after the face of God, groaning at God's silence, demanding his aid, and singing his glory, is me, the best of me and the worst of me.

I give thee thanks, O Lord, with my whole heart.
Psalm 138

Other prayers

There are of course, other prayers that one could refer to, the *Veni Sancte Spiritus*, the *Magnificat*, the *Memorare*, the *Angelus*, the Way of the Cross, and all the prayers that are included in the Mass, such as the *Kyrie*, the *Gloria* and the *Sanctus*. Here are four from the Old Testament.

Canticle of Hannah

Hannah exults the Lord who has fulfilled her desire of having a son. Some of her expressions are found in the *Magnificat*. Here are some verses of Hannah's canticle:

My heart exults in the Lord;
my strength is exalted in the Lord.
My mouth derides my enemies,
because I rejoice in thy salvation.

The bows of the mighty are broken,
but the feeble gird on strength.
Those who were full have hired
themselves out for bread,
but those who were hungry
have ceased to hunger.

The Lord kills and brings to life...
he brings low, he also exalts...

He raises up the poor from the dust;
he lifts the needy from the ash heap,
to make them sit with princes
and inherit a seat of honour.

cf. 1 Sam 2:1-8

A prayer of David

A real offering. David prays before the Lord.

"Who am I, O Lord God, and what is my house, that thou hast brought me thus far? And this was a small thing in thy eyes, O God; thou hast also spoken of thy servant's house for a great while to come, and hast shown me future generations, O Lord God! And what more can David say to thee for honouring thy servant? For thou knowest thy servant. For thy servant's sake, O Lord, and according to thy own heart, thou hast wrought all this greatness, in making known all these great things. There is none like thee, O Lord, and there is no God besides thee, according to all that we have heard with our ears. What other nation on earth is like thy people Israel, whom God went to redeem

Magnificat

**My heart praises
the Lord;
my soul is glad because
of God my Saviour,
for he has remembered
me, his lowly servant!
From now on all people
will call me happy,
because of the great
things the mighty God
has done for me.
His name is holy;
from one generation to
another he shows
mercy to those who
honour him.
He has stretched out
his mighty arm
and scattered the proud
with all their plans.
He has brought down
mighty kings from
their thrones,
and lifted up the lowly.
He has filled the hungry
with good things,
and sent the rich away
with empty hands.
He has kept the promise
he made to our
ancestors, and
has come to the help
of his servant Israel.
He has remembered
to show mercy
to Abraham and to all
his descendants
for ever!**

Good News Version

Lk 1:46-55

to be his people, making for thyself a name for great and terrible things, in driving out nations before thy people whom thou didst redeem from Egypt? And thou didst make thy people Israel to be thy people for ever; and thou, O Lord, didst become their God. And now, O Lord, let the word which thou hast spoken concerning thy servant and concerning his house be established for ever and do as thou hast spoken; and thy name will be established and magnified for ever, saying, 'The Lord of hosts, the God of Israel, is Israel's God,' and the house of thy servant David will be established before thee. For thou, my God, hast revealed to thy servant that thou wilt build a house for him; therefore thy servant has found courage to pray before thee. And now, O Lord, thou art God, and thou hast promised this good thing to thy servant; now therefore may it please thee to bless the house of thy servant, that it may continue for ever before thee; for what thou, O Lord, hast blessed is blessed for ever."

1 Chron 17:16-27

**Most High,
omnipotent,
good Lord,
to you praise,
glory and honour
and all benediction.
To you alone,
Most High,
do they belong,
and there is
no one worthy
to mention you.
Praised be my Lord,
by means of all your
creatures.**

St Francis of Assisi

Prayer of Solomon

A prayer for the transfer of the Ark of the Covenant, and above all, for obtaining wisdom:

With thee is wisdom, who knows thy works
and was present when thou didst make the world,
and who understands what is pleasing in thy sight
and what is right according to thy commandments.
Send her forth from the holy heaven
and from the throne of thy glory send her,
that she may be with me and toil,
and that I may learn what is pleasing to thee.

For she knows and understands all things,
and she will guide me wisely in my actions
and guard me with her glory.

Who has learned thy counsel,
unless thou hast given wisdom
and sent thy holy Spirit from on high?

And thus the paths of those on earth were set right,
and men were taught what pleases thee,
and were saved by wisdom.

Wisdom 9:9-11.17-18

The Canticle of the three young men in the furnace

Blessed art thou, O Lord, God of our fathers,
and to be praised and highly exalted for ever.

And blessed is thy glorious holy name
and to be highly exalted for ever.

Blessed art thou in the temple of thy holy glory
and to be extolled and highly glorified for ever.

Blessed are thou upon the throne of thy kingdom
and to be extolled and highly exalted forever.

Bless the Lord, nights and days.

Bless the Lord, light and darkness.

Bless the Lord, lightning and clouds.

Let the earth bless the Lord;
let it sing praise to him and highly exalt him for ever.

Bless the Lord, you servants of the Lord.

Bless the Lord, spirits and souls of the righteous.

Bless the Lord, you who are holy and humble in heart.

Dan 3:29-31.33.47-49.52.63-65

What's the use of praying?

The objections to prayer tend to blend into one another. These are the main ones:

I haven't got the time

This is a standard observation. There can be no doubt that modern life, which is all speed and noise and output and razzamatazz, doesn't leave much space for recollection. On the other hand, we find plenty of time for watching TV, or for eating up the miles in our cars. There's plenty of time for what you really like. If you look closely at the way you use your time, you'll find plenty of space; and nowadays we are more and more strongly aware of the need for silence and interiority, in a word, for prayer.

Trying to pray is praying. Never give up trying.

Cardinal Hume

The lack of time is a poor excuse, an alibi, especially when you consider that for lay-people we're not generally talking about hour after hour of prayer. Quite short stretches are all that are required, in the morning or in the evening, or if there's a moment during the day, or even on the bus. What matters is not the total score in minutes, but the quality of our presence to God, at all times and everywhere, and that our lives have a permanent atmosphere of prayer. But, obviously, in order to get to that state, we need to mark out various sacrosanct spaces in our lives, and make an effort to give them priority. These are means, of course, not

We are as strictly obliged to cling to God by action in the time of action as by prayer in its season.

Brother Lawrence

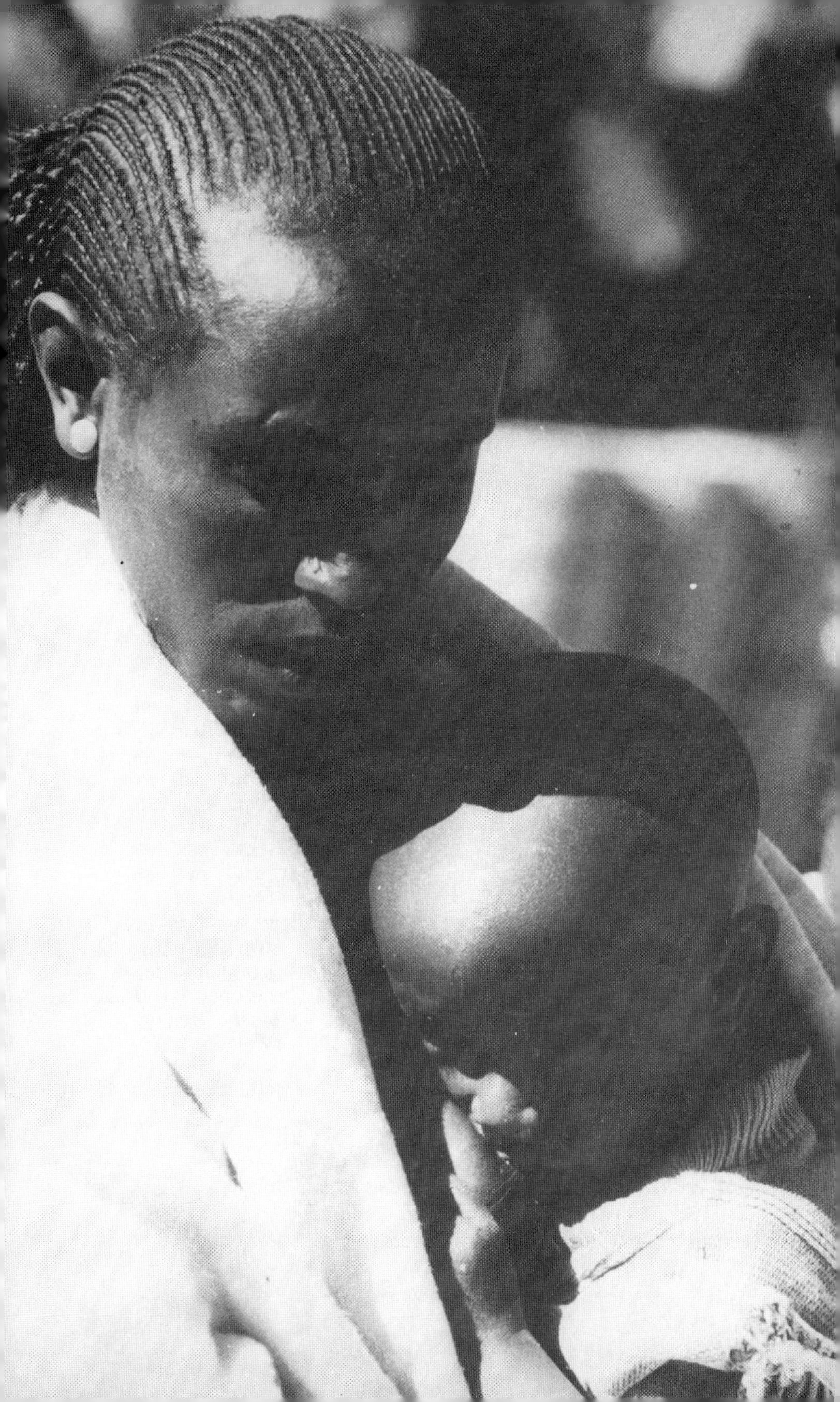

ends. Mother Teresa writes: "Prayer for me means becoming twenty-four hours a day at one with the will of Jesus, to live for him, through him, and with him."

I get distracted

Who doesn't? St Augustine himself said that if he had to pray without distractions, he didn't see "what hope would remain". And Thomas Aquinas, for his part, asserts that distractions "do not make prayer ineffective", because it remains an act of love.

You only learn to pray by praying.

St John Climacus (3rd century)

We must not suppose that distractions are an obstacle that you've absolutely got to blast away in order to have perfect concentration. The more I struggle against them, the more I actually risk reinforcing them. Why get all tensed up about them? Many spiritual directors suggest integrating them into the prayer, making them into occasions of prayer: a person that comes into my mind, or an anxiety that preoccupies me. Distractions, like lack of time, can be just an excuse or an alibi: the only thing to do is to treat them as a challenge; then, while our prayer may lose some of its unity, it will gain in richness.

If the face of God exercises its fascination on us, our activity will be renewed by his light, and even our setbacks become resurrections.
If you do not know the face of God through contemplation, you will not recognize it in action either, even when it shines out before you in the face of the victims and the lowly ones.

Hans Urs von Balthasar

God doesn't say anything

Are you waiting for him to have a private conversation with you, and to speak to you like you speak to him? We need to respect God's silence; that silence might be his way of replying, putting us face-to-face with ourselves, with no prattling. As it happens, God "speaks to us" in the Old Testament and in the New Testament; he speaks to us in

Jesus' life; he speaks to us through events in our lives, through the lives of the saints, and of all his Son's friends, which is to say, those who are attentive to his Spirit. It is really that we don't listen. We fail to make an area of silence within ourselves, and then we wait for "human" words, when, as a matter of fact, silence is also an expression of love, possibly more effective than words.

I can't stick at it

This is not really surprising. The greatest saints knew periods of weariness, desolation and aridity. There are the moments when you stop praying, you get discouraged, you even despair. Prayer is like the sea: you don't necessarily get an easy crossing; you can get becalmed, or you get a light breeze, or strong winds or gales. Père de Lubac wrote in his *Paradoxes*: "Those who have never seen the sea think that it's incredibly boring, but, in fact, nothing is more varied, or more packed with surprises. And, in our inner life, it's just like that with the contemplation of God".

With prayer you never make any definitive gains, nor any definitive losses. It's like life; or, rather, prayer is the heart of life, with its periods of growth, and its times of joy, of sickness, of fever, of depressions, with all its plans, its surprises, its deprivation and its abundance.

Prayer is an excuse for doing nothing

Is prayer just a matter of looking for shelter in a serene and hazard-free refuge? Well, it

**No one can separate
prayer and action.
It's neither struggle
nor contemplation,
but the two together,
the one bursting forth
from the other.
The Risen One
is by your side
wherever you go,
not only in church,
but also in the street,
and at work.
Contemplation
doesn't mean
shutting our eyes
in the face of all
that threatens or
attacks the weak
ones of this world, or
blinkering ourselves
to the sin that is war.
Contemplation is a
peaceful power which
works on you and
hollows you out.**

Brother Roger of Taizé

can be, but generally it's not. Prayer is not a quick answer, nor does it dispense us from action.

When Therese of Lisieux retired into the Carmelite monastery in order to pray she did not retire from the world's preoccupations. On the contrary, she carried them with her, in the depths of her heart, whether it was a spectacular crime or some apostolic work beyond her normal horizon. Who would have the nerve to call her either uncaring or useless? She has, after all, been made patron saint of the Missions.

Prayer is, in fact, an adventure, or a struggle, more testing than ordinary fighting, for the opponents are darkness and temptation, and evil in all its forms. Peguy said that "the real revolutionaries are those with an inner life". Prayer prevents action from becoming mindless. It roots it in our hearts, in the peace of the depths of our being.

The Carmelite Sisters at Mazille, France, claim: "It is our view that you can only do something significant if your heart beats deep inside the world... If prayer is the place where our recognition of God meets our recognition of our fellow-humans, then it becomes action. It makes us take part in the battle

There is but one way that leads to God and that is prayer. If anyone tells you another they are deceiving you.

St Teresa of Avila

Prayer is not a flight from reality, nor a side-stepping for "our" daily bread. I must myself give this bread to those who have none... If I pray for peace, I must commit myself to working for peace. Prayer is not "pie in the sky": we can only pray if we take full responsibility for what we say, and it is only then that we can really experience for ourselves God's power and his initiative as we pray.

Cardinal Roger Etchegaray

that is being fought in the world, the battle for the new order of things that Christ proclaimed".

Work is prayer

If this means that work can take the place of prayer, it is simply false. Work can, of course, be a prayer, if it is done in this spirit, if it is charged with prayerfulness in some way. But it can also be a perfectly neutral activity, with no spiritual significance, whatever its nobility or generosity, however wonderful its effect.

Some people make an additional point, that prayer is the vocation of hermits and contemplatives and monks and nuns, while the laity look after the temporal side of things, so that there is a kind of division of responsibilities. This assumes that lay-people are not themselves summoned to prayer. But they need it just as much as (perhaps more than) those who consecrate their whole lives to it. Obviously there are differences, in the content of prayer, for example, or in life-styles, or in religious status, but we are all called to pray.

God is not of the order of means to an end, a way of making up what we lack. He is Someone.

Pope John Paul II

What good does it do?

"Prayer changes nothing: look at all the injustice there is, all the wars, and how much misery and how much innocent suffering there is in the world. With all the advances in science, we know what makes the world go round: there is no more room for God, and therefore no more room for prayer. Isn't it true that there's less and less prayer nowadays? Prayer looks like a useless luxury."

First of all, it depends on the image you have of God. His power is not going to change the course of the world or meet our desires and expectations with a wave of a magic wand. God is a source, not a power; he is a presence, not a mechanic. He is no "good" for anything, in the utilitarian sense. God is the heart of our heart. He is love and forgiveness; he is what we most need in order to live in love, to find happiness and peace on earth. He is himself happiness and peace.

It is to remind us of himself that he sent Jesus to us, and we have to continue what Jesus did. So God's action comes through our action, our presence to him and to others. Cardinal Marty wrote: "When I was in the seminary, they taught me that prayer was the counterweight to action. It is more than that: it is the weight of action." Or, as Jean Sulivan says: "Prayer radically changes the way we exist, and our manner of being present in the world. It changes the world by changing us."

And what about children?

The most important time to learn to pray is in childhood. Prayer and childhood go hand-in-hand, for children have a better instinct for prayer than adults, and all you have to do is help them to get it going, get them to express themselves without putting them down or discouraging them, or making them into child prodigies, whose thoughts or reflections get repeated with a superior smile.

Are families praying less together? Nowadays parents are not always free at the same times as their children. And there is of course the

Dear God, I like birthdays even when they are not my own, because everyone is happy. I like giving people presents. At Christmas what do you celebrate most – your birthday or Christmas?

Matthew (aged 10)

problem of finding a style of prayer that is not too difficult for the children and too childish for the adults. Different families have different formulae: sometimes you will have the parents praying on their own, at other times with the 3-7 year-olds, and again at other times with the 8-12 year-olds. And, of course, the young want more say in it.

When you ask around, the striking thing is how much spontaneity there is and how much flexibility. Sometimes prayer starts from what has happened during the day, or what is going on in the world. Or the starting-point might be a gospel story or a feast-day, or a book, a film, or the countryside, or a monument that people have visited. As they talk, it becomes prayer. There are different styles and different rhythms. People might sing. This flexibility is, of course, much more demanding than doing the same things every day, and requires preparation.

Praying with a child means listening to what is already inside him, and to what could set him praying. It may also involve getting hold of books or cassettes: there is plenty of material.

Parents sometimes want to be given proper children's prayers, which they can give to the children in their turn. They do exist, but in fact children are perfectly capable of making up their own prayers, often with greater ease (and greater success) than adults.

7
The sources of prayer

When we experience difficulties in prayer, it is sometimes because we have not drawn sufficiently on the sources of prayer.

The Eucharist: the highest form of prayer

People are too inclined to drive a wedge between the Eucharistic Prayer and what you might call ordinary prayer, whether private or shared. The Mass is undeniably the highest form of prayer, but there is a danger of not participating properly in it if it has no bedrock in the rest of our lives. Prayer leads us naturally into the Eucharistic celebration which links us with Christ's thanksgiving to his Father; and the Mass sends us back into ordinary everyday prayer.

It is truly right
and just, it is fitting
to the limitless
splendour of
your holiness,
Oh one true God,
to praise you,
to bless you,
to adore you,
to sing your grace
and your glory;
to offer you, from
a broken heart,
in the spirit of the
poor, this spiritual
offering, to gain
revelation of
the truth.

Byzantine Liturgy of St Basil

In the Mass you find all sorts of prayers, which we have distinguished for the purposes of this discussion, but which cannot really be separated, and which are fused into a single whole at Mass: thanksgiving, which is really the basis of other types of prayer, such as asking pardon (as in the *Kyrie*, for example), petition (the prayers after the Consecration), praise (at the *Sanctus* and elsewhere), adoration (especially after the words of Institution).

Another link between daily prayer and its high point in the Eucharist is the Lord's

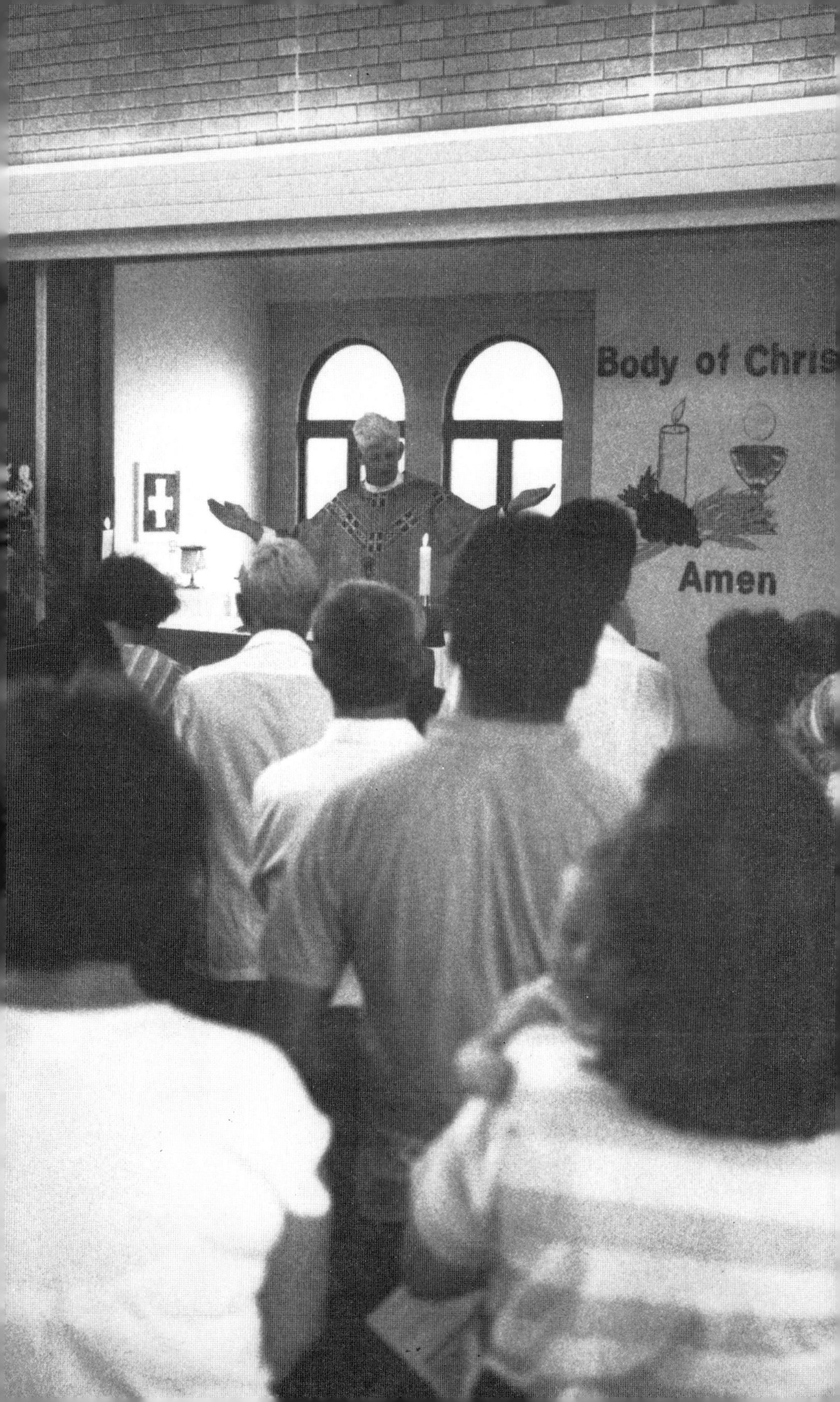

Body of Chris
Amen

Prayer, an everyday prayer which takes on a new dimension in the Mass.

At Mass, we may say, our prayers are seen in their community or Church setting (one might almost call it "cosmic", as Teilhard de Chardin does).

We may doubt if it is possible to live a life of prayer without summing it up in the Eucharist, while, on the other hand, the Eucharist, valid as it may be in itself, can hardly bear fruit in our lives if it is merely a parenthesis, albeit a very beautiful one.

The gospel is a book to pray through

Reading the Good News is an essential step for the Christian, but its message needs to be prayed over if it is to take root in our hearts. For the gospel isn't just a message to ponder on, or a teaching that we have to study; it is Someone to love. Prayer is the act that consummates this personal relationship. So the gospel is one of the sources of prayer.

How do you go about transforming this message into prayer? The parables are particularly good for this, as they illustrate the Beatitudes and tell us what the kingdom is like. Jesus lives, then, and acts them out: he is the Good Samaritan; he is the Shepherd looking for the lost sheep; he is the "prodigal Father".

And what about me? Am I not the lost sheep that asks Jesus to come and find it? Or one of those weeds that take root everywhere except in the Lord?

Scripture is the source of life... From it spring up and flow rivers which irrigate all the regions of the Church. Christians not only drink from this source in the liturgy, but from it receive a water channel. If they continue with the reading and let it overflow through contemplation; one day they will find a clear, deep lake within themselves in which heaven is reflected.

L. Alonso Schökel

Père Bro suggests that we choose from the gospel the principal moments of Christ's life and re-read them from the perspective of the Lord's Prayer. He asks us to find out what this prayer means for us at this particular moment of Christ's life.

The gospel is one of the great sources of prayer, and so are the books of Holy Scripture – Old and New Testament – in which the saving action and living Word of God are expressed by the Spirit of God.

The official prayer of the Church

All through the centuries there has been a "liturgical thread" made up of psalms, hymns, readings and actions. This prayer more or less follows the rhythms of the day (at least morning and evening) and of the year. It started with Christian communities who used it with great freedom, and then spread to parishes and dioceses; then the monks modified it and gave it structure, and they still use it and sing it.

So it became the priest's breviary, and subsequently it got shortened and better adapted to modern conditions, and made suitable for individual use. The final stage is the modern "Liturgy of the Hours", equally suitable for use by laity or priests, alone or in common.

Some people find this kind of prayer quite difficult, because it draws so heavily on the psalms, which can be disconcerting, and not always clearly relevant to our contemporary anxieties. But many individuals and communities find that they can fit in quite well, and that this form of prayer helps them in their

Praise the Lord!
Praise God in his sanctuary;
praise him in his mighty firmament!

Praise him for his mighty deeds;
praise him according to his exceeding greatness!

Praise him with the sound of trumpets;
praise him with lute and harp!

Praise him with timbrel and dance;
praise him with strings and pipe!

Praise him with sounding of cymbals;
praise him with loud clashing cymbals!

Let everything that breathes praise the Lord!
Praise the Lord!

Psalm 150

renewal, keeps them present to the world, and provides a kind of continuity that is independent of individual peaks and troughs. Using this form of prayer, people can take part in the Church's prayer on their own, because it is the common form of prayer (despite one or two cultural modifications).

There is occasionally a mistaken tendency to oppose liturgical and private or spontaneous prayer: each can in fact help the other. Some missals, for instance, contain prayers that are not properly speaking liturgical.

The sacraments, which are a part of the Church's liturgy, are likewise sources of prayer. They may be described as moments of prayer and the means whereby a relationship with Father, Son and Holy Spirit is established. They cannot be separated from the prayer with which they are surrounded (and should be even more surrounded).

The treasury of prayer

Finally, we should never forget that outside of the liturgy there exists an extraordinary reservoir of prayer which has built up over the centuries and which goes from the prayer of the earliest Christians right down to those of the present day. We do not know this gold mine well enough (though there are nowadays books and publications to help us, e.g., *The Treasury of the Holy Spirit, The Oxford Book of Prayer, Words of Wisdom*).

Formal prayers are ours to use at will, according to our needs. More than this, they are invitations to express ourselves in prayer. This treasury, stored up over the centuries, is not closed or restricted to museums: it is

Some short prayers:

Lord, be not far from me.

Psalm 35:22

Lord, show me your face.

Exodus 33:18

Lord, you know I love you.

John 21:15

Lord,
come to my aid.

Matthew 15:25

Lord, increase my faith.

Luke 17:5

Lord, I give you everything.

Pascal

alive, the tip of the iceberg of that great and holy treasury of the people of God. Why should we not make our own contribution?

The prayer of the heart

In the Eastern Church, where it is much more widely practised than in the West, it is called: "Jesus Prayer". It goes back to the desert Fathers, and practised in Russia from the fifteenth century. It is also known as: *philocalia* or *hesychasm,* but it is the simplest form of prayer: the invocation of the name of Jesus. Sometimes it is developed into a phrase, half of which is breathed out, and the other half is breathed in.

The best known formula is: "Lord Jesus Christ, Son of God, have mercy on me, a sinner". The ideal is to repeat it indefinitely. Short as it is, it is quite complete. It attests to Christ's Incarnation, and unites us to him, and through him to the Church and to all humanity. It is a profession of faith, but to live out that faith we need to recognise that we are sinners.

Obviously it is difficult to say it for a long time with 100% attention, unless you're a monk or a hermit (and even then!). But it acts as a constant reminder, the insistent ticking of a clock, an unending groundswell which colours our life and gives it direction, with all the power (and the perils) that repetition can bring.

This side of words

We are used, from our schooldays onwards, to expressing ourselves in words. And relig-

People think
they do not know
how to pray.
Ultimately that's
not important,
because God
understands our
sighs,and knows
what our silence
means.
Silence is the whole
of prayer:
God speaks to us,
breathing silently;
he touches us
in that aloneness
that no other human
can fill.

Brother Roger of Taizé

ion too can be invaded by words. You can pray with words, but are there no other ways of encountering God, no other sources of prayer?

Simple silence

A word of warning: there are different kinds of silence. There is a silence that is burdensome refusal or fearfulness. And there is a peaceful silence that denotes attentive listening. This is a fulfilled silence, "the walled garden where alone the soul can meet its God".

So we can distinguish three stages: first, the silence which is the absence of noise. This is a negative sort of silence, but it has its uses. Then there is the silence you get when, for the moment at least, you have managed to cut out that inner cinema and the heart's creaking: the absence of trouble. But deeper yet is the silence of presence – and the one who is present is the God whom we have rediscovered waiting for us. This silence speaks wordlessly. Words can get in the way of what is deeply personal and unconditioned. People who love each other reach a point where they understand each other and love each other without saying a word. The Other is there, and we enter into communication. This silence is the silence of contemplation and adoration.

Silence is not simply negation but presence of the Beloved.

Maria Boulding

Why are we afraid of silence? Without silence, our apostolate, our preaching, our busy-ness and even our prayer, can die of a surfeit of words. This silence is only obtained at a price; some asceticism is required. No force is needed, only patience, and, as with all sorts of prayer, humility, perseverance, confidence and listening.

Using images

Images too can be a source of prayer, and it is not even necessary to put into words the contemplation that they give rise to.

What images? Cathedral carvings (which are prayerful retellings of the Bible stories), wooden sculptures, paintings like the works of Giotto or Fra Angelico, the frescoes of St Sabina, the ceiling of the Sistine Chapel, paintings, even photographs: landscapes, or children's faces, for instance.

Icons ought to get a special mention. Part of the rich heritage of the Eastern Church they are themselves prayer, "windows to heaven" through which we contemplate the mysteries of the kingdom.

**The icon is Christ,
the God made
visible;
it is the image of
the Mother of God
and of all who have
been transformed
by grace.
These friends of God
are my friends
and I belong
to them.**

Oliver Clement

With flowers

"Say it with flowers." We do it for important days like birthdays: why not also for the Lord? When words fail, flowers take up the attempt to utter what is beyond words.

With my body

You can use your body in prayer: standing up, leaning over, on your knees, prostrate, with raised hands... So the body is a kind of instrument in prayer. Sometimes, of course, this can just be reduced to a technique, especially in the East, and indeed a spirituality very foreign to our own. However, if there is sometimes a danger there, we should never forget that it may be important to integrate the body (even by the use of dance) in an approach to prayer. There is a particular strand in spirituality that has tended too much towards mistrust of the body.

**Dance allows us to
prolong anything:
thoughts, gestures,
feelings.
Living in unity with
the Spirit of Jesus
reconciles body
and soul.
That is why dance
can be an instrument
of prayer, a moving
and mobile way of
expressing praise
to God.**

Mireille Negre

The advice of Jesus

The pieces of advice given by Jesus inspired by behaviour he noticed in the Temple or the synagogue: they are "things seen". Can we say they are not relevant today?

Be reconciled

If you are offering your gift at the altar, and there remember that your brother has something against you, leave your gift there before the altar and go; first be reconciled to your brother, and then come and offer your gift.

Mt 5:23-24

We would say today: when you go to church to pray or to take part in the Eucharist, be sure that you are not in any conflict with your brother, or whoever it might be. Don't wait till he comes to see you. Make the first move. Otherwise there is no real prayer. But if you are the one who has something against someone, how much more should you do this.

Blessed rather are those who hear the word of God and keep it!

Luke 11:28

And whenever you stand praying, forgive, if you have anything against any one; so that your Father also who is in heaven may forgive you your trespasses.

Mk 11:25

Pray in secret

And when you pray, you must not be like the hyprocrites; for they love to stand and pray in the synagogues and at the street corners, that they may be seen by men. Truly, I say to you, they have their reward. But when you pray, go into your room and shut the door and pray to your Father who is in secret; and your Father who sees in secret will reward you.

Mt 6:5-6

Is this to say you should only ever pray in your room, in solitude? By no means. Jesus left the crowd in order to pray. It is necessary at times. But here, in the context, "pray in secret" means to pray in the secret of the heart; there alone can we encounter God, as a son meets his father.

And as for that in the good soil, they are those who, hearing the word, hold it fast in an honest and good heart, and bring forth fruit with patience.

Luke 8:15

And Mary kept all these things in her heart.

Luke 2:51

Be trustful

Ask, and it will be given you; seek, and you will find; knock, and it will be opened to you. For every one who asks receives, and he who seeks finds, and to him who knocks it will be opened. Or what man of you, if his son asks him for bread, will give him a stone?

Mt 6:7-9

This advice follows the two other examples in Matthew's text. And all three precede the "Our Father". They are therefore very important, since the "Our Father" is the ideal Christian prayer. The quality of a prayer is not measured by its length and its repetitions (cf. also Mk 12:40, where Jesus denounces "those who make a show of saying long prayers").

The worst thing is to give up...
Even though we walk with tiny steps, falling, getting up again, when we keep walking and going forward we arrive, although late, at the goal.

Teresa of Avila

True prayer is measured by its filial trust, which inspires the "Our Father".

Be humble

He also told this parable to some who trusted in themselves that they were righteous and despised others: "Two men went up into the temple to pray, one a Pharisee and the other a tax collector. The Pharisee stood and prayed thus with himself, 'God, I thank thee that I am not like other men, extortioners, unjust, adulterers, or even like this tax collector. I fast twice a week, I give tithes of all that I get.' But the tax collector, standing far off, would not even lift up his eyes to heaven, but beat his breast, saying, 'God, be merciful to me a sinner!'"

Lk 18:9-13

The infinitely loving one is infinitely poor, infinitely humble, infinitely dependent.

François Varillon

Jesus is looking at the behaviour of the Jews in the Temple, especially the Pharisees, who believe themselves to be better than the rest. What kind of relationship can we have with God the Father if we come before him burdened with pride, with no consciousness of being sinners? Still the filial relationship.

At all times

Take heed to yourselves lest your hearts be weighed down with dissipation and drunkenness and cares of this life, and that day come upon you suddenly like a snare; for it will come upon all who dwell upon the face of the whole earth. But watch at all times, praying that you may have strength to escape all these things that will take place, and to stand before the Son of man.

Lk 21:34-36

Pray without ceasing, and live in the love of the Lord, loved in the beloved, preserved in the living, saved in him who has been redeemed, and you will be found incorruptible throughout the ages, in the name of your Father. Alleluia!

Ancient exhortation

That day means the day of Judgement, the day of the end of the world. But the day when everything stops also means the day of our death, which can happen at any moment. Hence the advice to watch and pray "at all times".

Together

Again I say to you, if two of you agree on earth about anything they ask, it will be done for them by my Father in heaven. For where two or three are gathered in my name, there am I in the midst of them.

Mt 18:19-20

The choice is not between solitary prayer and shared prayer. Both are needed. What counts, once again, is to pray to the Father, in the name of the Son.

**Pray in hope,
pray with faith
and love,
pray with
perseverance
and patience,
pray like
a poor man.**

***St Augustine
Letter to Proba***

Without growing up

Two parables here, that of the importunate friend (insisting on making you open the door at night) just after the "Our Father" (Lk 11:5-8) and that of the importunate widow (who ends up making the judge give her justice, by her insistence [Lk 18:1-5]).

In both these parables there is one instruction, very clear and very simple: "Pray without ceasing and without becoming discouraged." If it is true with regard to a friend or a judge, how much more so with regard to God! Not at all because he wants us to importune him to make him respond, but because our insistence is the sign of our faith. This is true of our asking and also of our thanksgiving: "Let prayer keep you vigilant in thanksgiving," said St Paul (Col 4:2) and "On every occasion, have recourse to supplication and prayer, combined with thanksgiving, in presenting your requests to God."

Prayers of blessing

The Bible is full of prayers of blessing, expressions of gratitude to God. Parents blessed their children; Jesus blessed the Father continuously, touching everybody with grace. Today we need to rediscover the lost art of blessing.

May the Lord bless you and keep you.
May his face shine upon you and
be gracious to you.
May he look upon you with kindness,
and give you his peace.

Numbers 6:24-26

May the road rise to meet you.
May the wind be always
at your back.
May the sun shine warm
upon your face,
the rain fall soft
upon your fields
and, until we meet again,
may God hold you
in the palm of his hand.

An Irish blessing

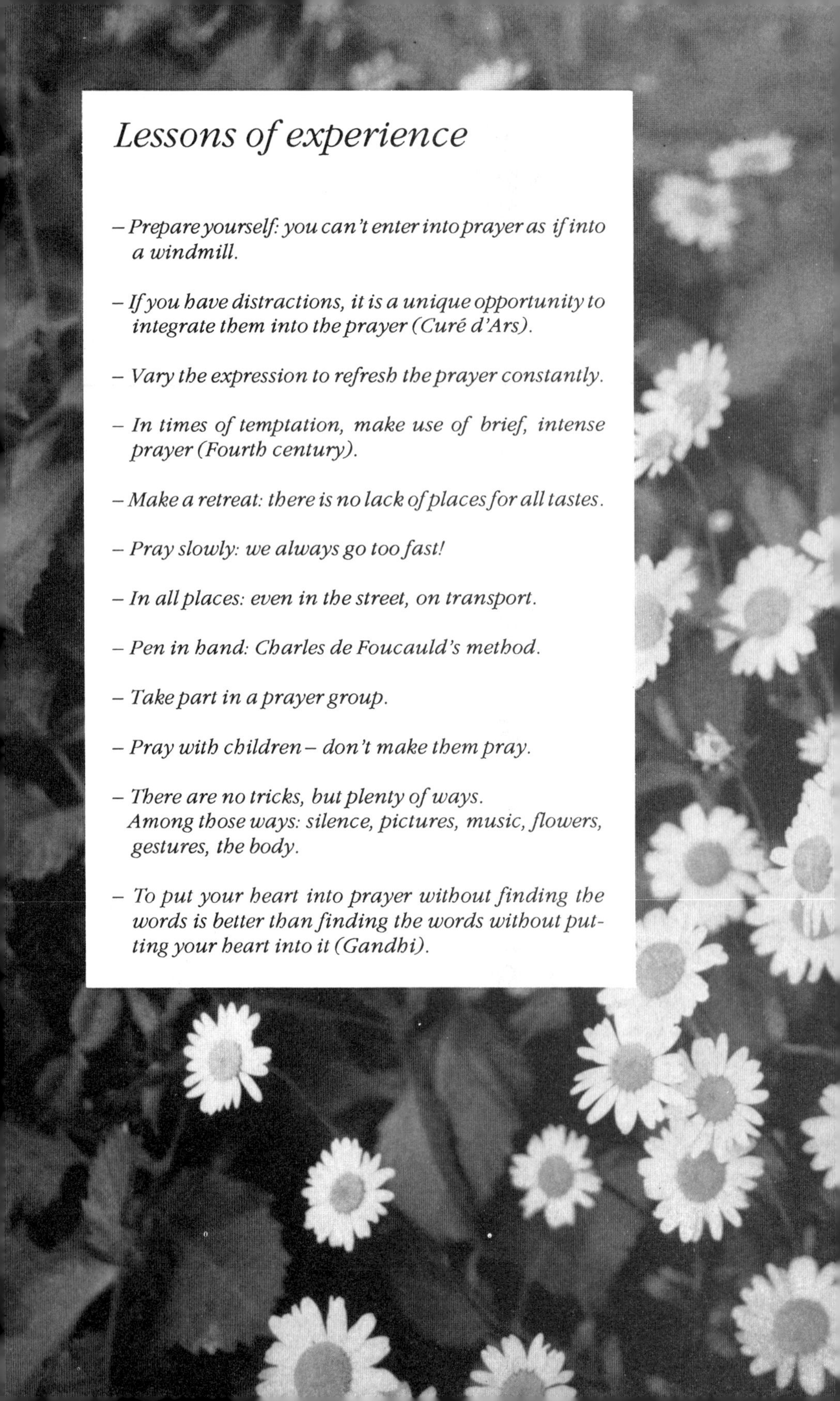

Lessons of experience

– *Prepare yourself: you can't enter into prayer as if into a windmill.*

– *If you have distractions, it is a unique opportunity to integrate them into the prayer (Curé d'Ars).*

– *Vary the expression to refresh the prayer constantly.*

– *In times of temptation, make use of brief, intense prayer (Fourth century).*

– *Make a retreat: there is no lack of places for all tastes.*

– *Pray slowly: we always go too fast!*

– *In all places: even in the street, on transport.*

– *Pen in hand: Charles de Foucauld's method.*

– *Take part in a prayer group.*

– *Pray with children – don't make them pray.*

– *There are no tricks, but plenty of ways.*
Among those ways: silence, pictures, music, flowers, gestures, the body.

– *To put your heart into prayer without finding the words is better than finding the words without putting your heart into it (Gandhi).*

Resources

by James Hanvey SJ

Some basic points – just to remember

1. There is no one who cannot pray. Prayer is the work of the Holy Spirit and it is the gift which we all have from baptism. Every time we pray – whether we feel that this is "good" or "bad" – is a living of that reality.

2. We never pray on our own. Although there may be many times when there is just ourselves, our prayer is always part of a great sea of prayer which is the reality of the Spirit in the Church. Our prayer flows from and to this sea of space and time but transcends it. Our prayer is part of the mystery of prayer taking place in every moment of our lives. Our prayer is always part of the continual prayer of all the saints. I may be praying but it is never "my" prayer.

Prayer is the meeting point of two desires: man's desire with God's desire, or rather the assumption of man's desire into God's desire.

Patrick Jaquemont

3. Number 2 means that no prayer is ever too small or too hurried or too poor. Remember the widow's mite.

4. Prayer is always something to be "done" not just thought about.

5. Prayer is always in the world; in this world. You can pray anywhere at any time in any mood or any state. Silence, scripture, images, flowers, gestures, memories.

6. There are many different schools of prayer but there are only two things really necessary: faith – or at least enough faith to try – and honesty – or at least a willingness to let God teach me that I don't have to fear to be honest.

7. Nature has its seasons, so does prayer. Prayer will change with changes in my life. Each season has its own challenge and its own beauty – each season has its own prayer.

8. The sacraments, especially the Eucharist, are the fountains of the life of prayer in the Church. As well as drinking from them or just being present at them you can take their prayers and make them your own. Read these prayers slowly and meditate on them.

9. Why not make a retreat?

Books on prayer

There are a great many books on spirituality and prayer. This is not an exhaustive bibliography. It is just some suggestions for beginning or continuing...

To pray,
in the infinitive.
Like to walk, to sing,
to read, to go.
Like to breathe,
above all.
Prayer is breathing.
And can one not
breathe?

Practical books on prayer:

The God of Surprises, G.W. Hughes, DLT, London 1985.
Silent Music, William Johnston, Fontana, Glasgow 1974.
Being in Love, William Johnston, Collins, Glasgow 1988.
Sadhana: a way to God, A. de Mello, Image, New York 1978.
The Prayer of Faith, Leonard Boase, Chapman, London 1962.
Prayer: Letters to Malcolm, C.S. Lewis, Fontana, Glasgow 1968.
Simple Prayer, J. Dalrymple, DLT, London

Maria Press, Indiana 1979.
Encounters with Silence, K. Rahner, Burns & Oates, London 1978.
The Oxford Book of Prayer, G. Appleton (ed.), Oxford University Press, Oxford 1985. [A selection of prayer in different traditions and for different occasions.]
Lord, teach me to pray, Jean-Guy Paradis, St Paul Publications, Slough.
Teach me to pray, St Paul Publications, Slough.

Classics:

The Confessions of St Augustine, Penguin Classics, London 1970.
St Teresa of Avila – A Life, Teresa of Avila, Penguin 1958.
Autobiography, Teresa of Avila, R.A. Knox (tr.), Harvill Press, 1958.
The Revelations of Divine Love, Julian of Norwich, Penguin Classics, 1966.
The Cloud of Unknowing, Penguin Classics, 1966.
The Imitation of Christ, Thomas à Kempis, R. Knox/M. Oakley (trs.), Burns & Oates, London 1959; Penguin Classics, 1975; Fontana, 1963.

We need silence in the clamour of life; we need contemplation in this agitation; we need communication in this show. We need truth, humility, hope. We need God.

Studies:

A History of Christian Spirituality (3 vols.), L. Bouyer et al. (eds.), Burns & Oates, London 1982.
The Study of Spirituality, C. Jones/G. Wainwright/E. Yarnold SJ (eds.), SPCK, London 1986.
The Wound of Knowledge, Rowan Williams, DLT, London 1979.
The God Within, [the mystical tradition of Northern Europe], Oliver Davies, DLT, London 1988.

You can live
for a few days
without eating,
but not without praying.
Prayer
is the key of the morning
and the bolt of the evening.
Prayer
is a sacred alliance
between
God and man.

Gandhi